IGUANAS

Darla Duhaime

Rourke
Educational Media

rourkeeducationalmedia.com

Before & After Reading Activities

Teaching Focus
Reading Comprehension- Have students find capital letters and punctuation in a sentence. Ask students to explain the purpose for using them in a sentence.

Before Reading:

Building Academic Vocabulary and Background Knowledge
Before reading a book, it is important to set the stage for your child or student by using pre-reading strategies. This will help them develop their vocabulary, increase their reading comprehension, and make connections across the curriculum.

1. Read the title and look at the cover. Let's make predictions about what this book will be about.
2. Take a picture walk by talking about the pictures/photographs in the book. Implant the vocabulary as you take the picture walk. Be sure to talk about the text features such as headings, Table of Contents, glossary, bolded words, captions, charts/diagrams, or Index.
3. Have students read the first page of text with you then have students read the remaining text.
4. Strategy Talk – use to assist students while reading.
    - Get your mouth ready
    - Look at the picture
    - Think…does it make sense
    - Think…does it look right
    - Think…does it sound right
    - Chunk it – by looking for a part you know
5. Read it again.

Content Area Vocabulary
Use glossary words in a sentence.

burrows
hatch
internal organs
predators

After Reading:

Comprehension and Extension Activity
After reading the book, work on the following questions with your child or students in order to check their level of reading comprehension and content mastery.

1. What are three things all reptiles have in common? (Summarize)
2. What does an iguana's skin help it do? (Asking Questions)
3. Name two things that make you different from reptiles. (Text to self connection)
4. Why do iguanas' tails break off? (Asking Questions)

Extension Activity
With an adult's permission, visit www.first-school.ws/puzzlesonline/animals/iguana.htm and complete the online iguana jigsaw puzzle. How quickly did you put it together?

Table of Contents

Iguanas are Reptiles   4
Baby Iguanas   16
Picture Glossary   23
Index   24
Websites to Visit   24
About the Author   24

Iguanas Are Reptiles

Reptiles are cold blooded. A reptile's body cannot make its own warmth.

5

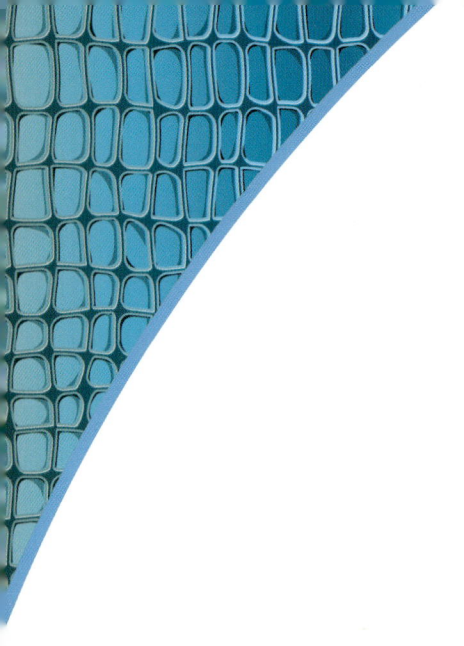

Iguanas are reptiles. Are they cold blooded?

7

8

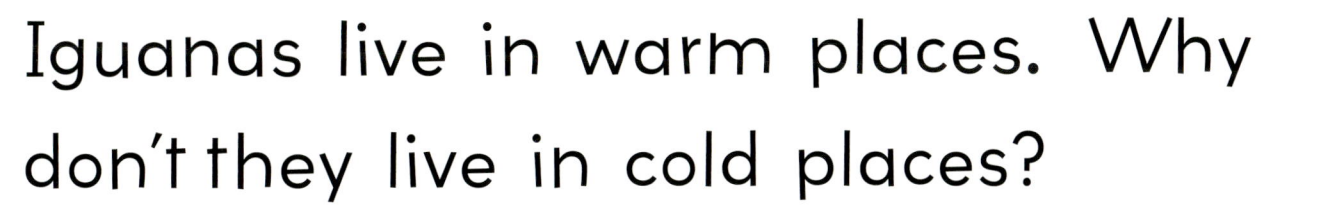

Iguanas live in warm places. Why don't they live in cold places?

skin

Reptiles have dry, scaly skin. What kind of skin does an iguana have?

An iguana's skin color helps it hide from **predators.**

13

burrow

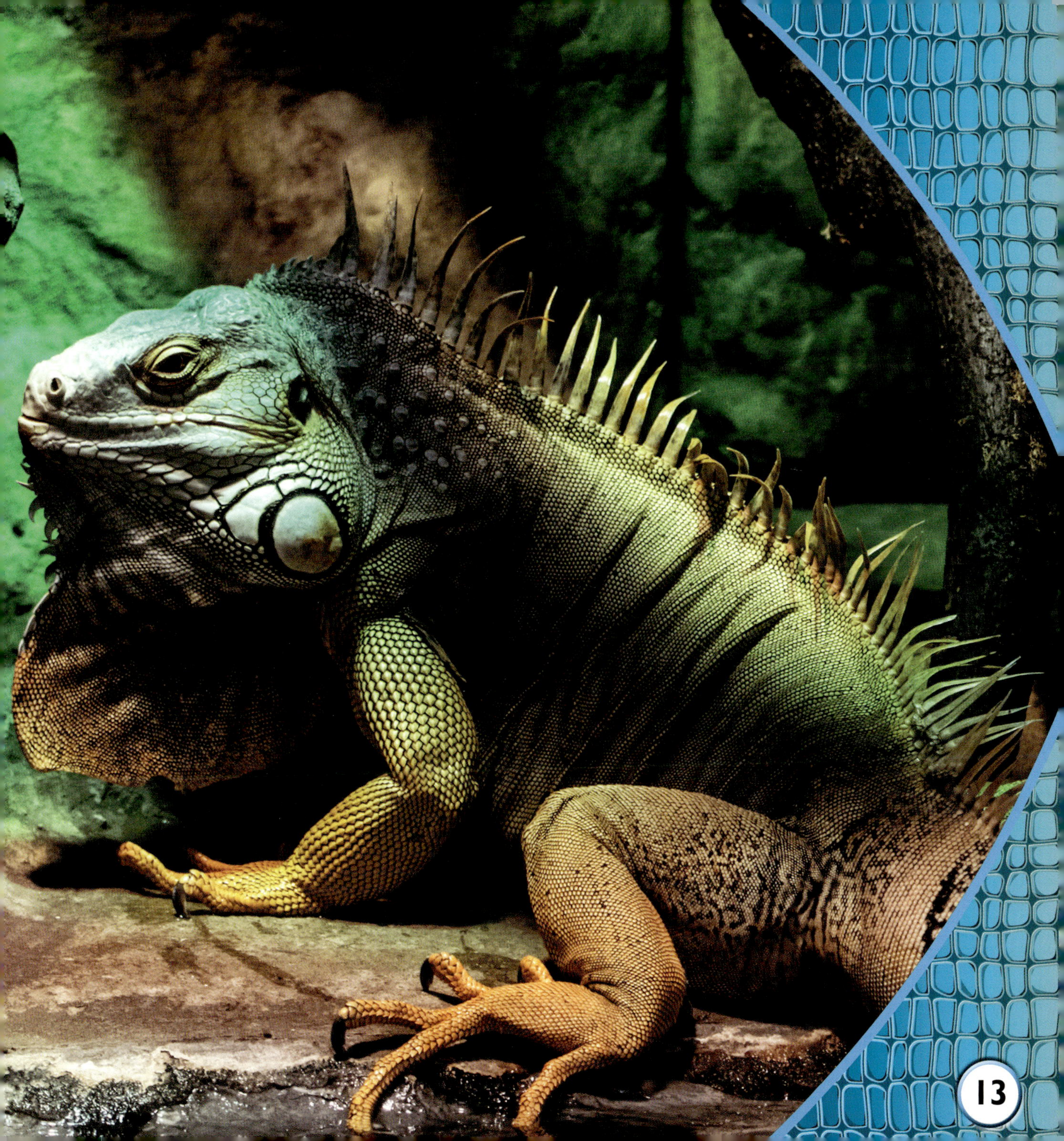

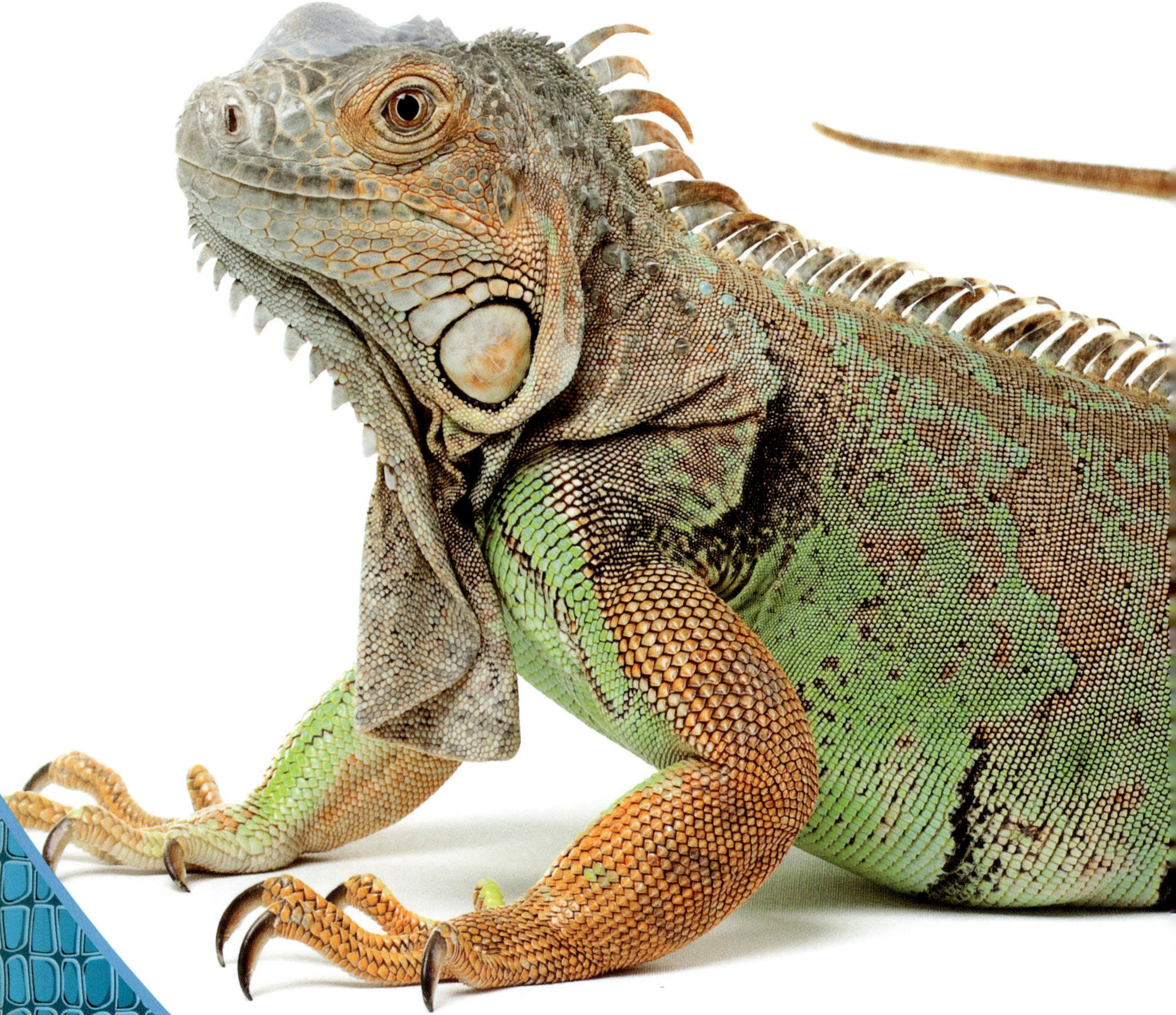

Reptiles have tails. An iguana's tail breaks off if it is grabbed by a predator. It grows back right away.

tail

Baby Iguanas

Most reptiles lay eggs. Do iguanas lay eggs?

egg

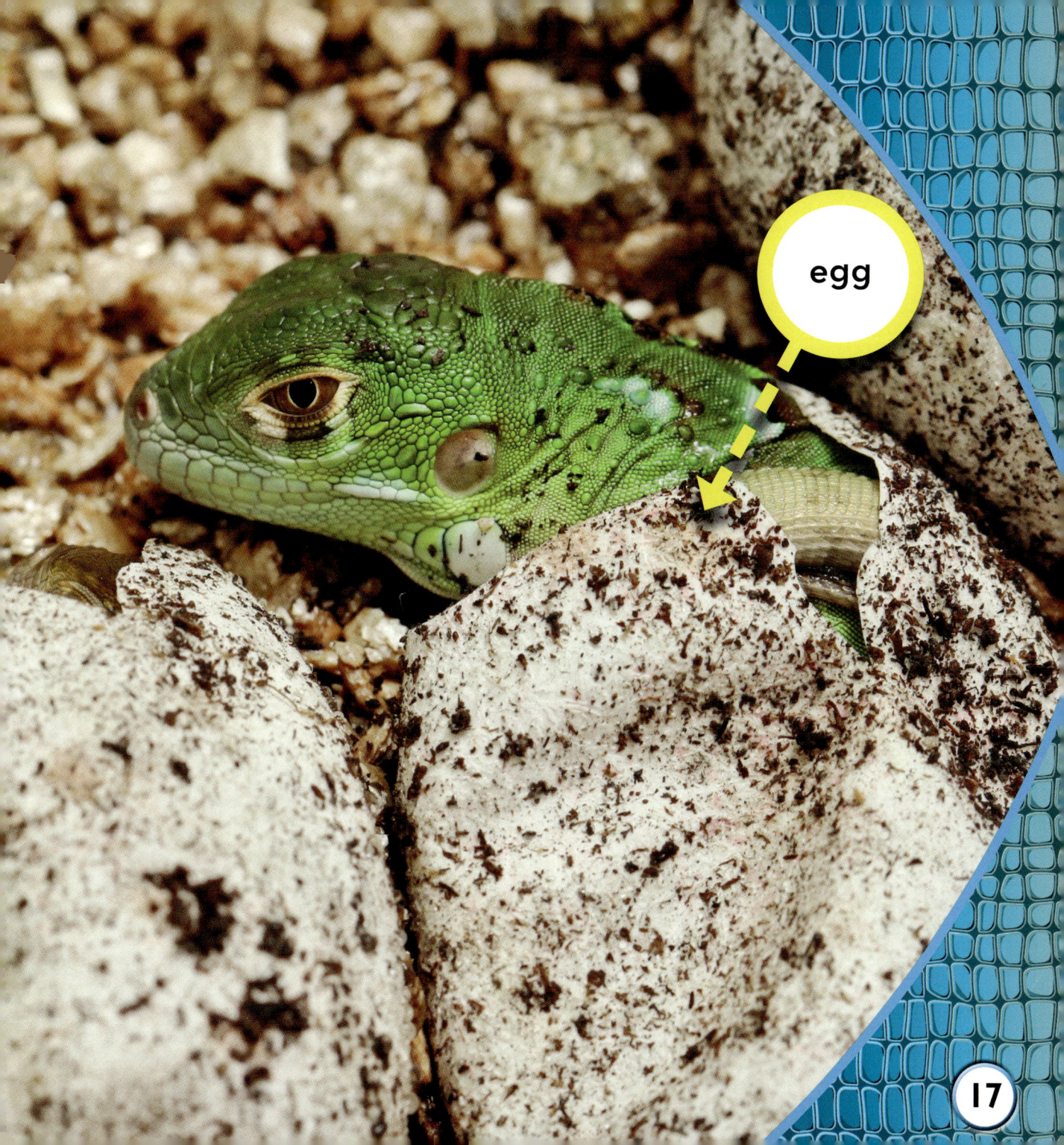

burrow

Iguanas lay their eggs inside **burrows**. When the babies **hatch**, they dig their way out.

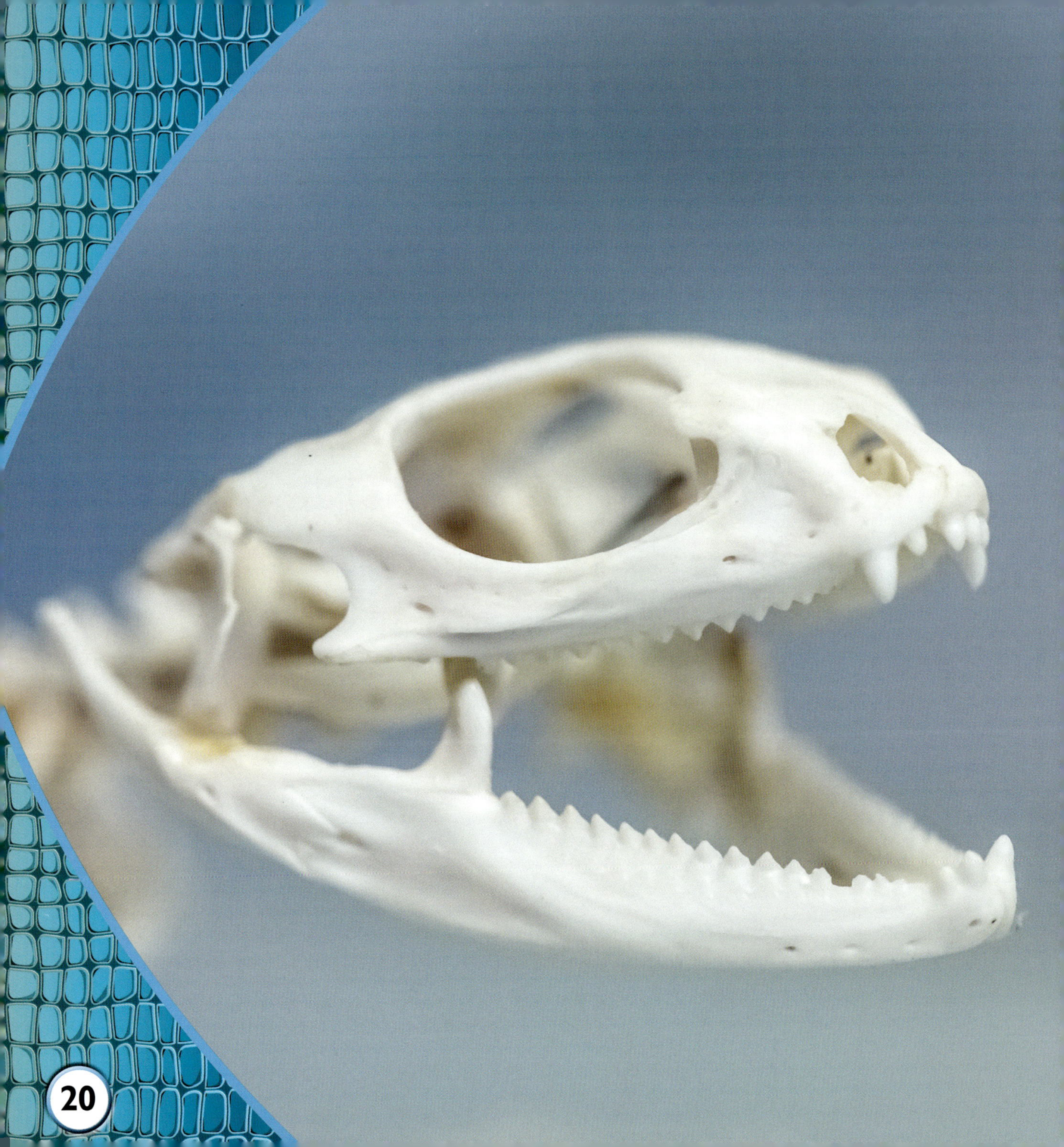

Reptiles have skeletons made of bones. An iguana's skeleton protects its **internal organs.**

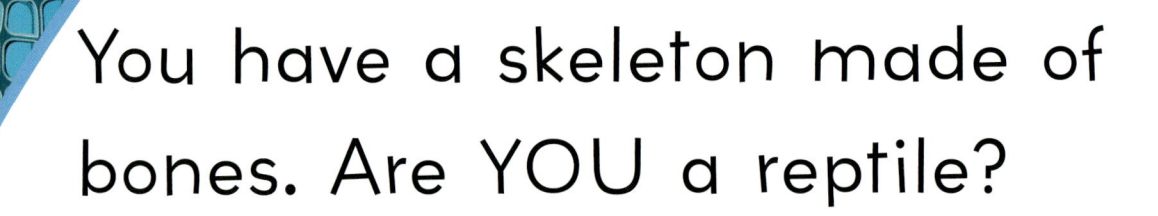

You have a skeleton made of bones. Are YOU a reptile?

Picture Glossary

burrows (BUR-ohs): Tunnels or holes in the ground made by animals.

hatch (hatch): When an egg hatches, it breaks open and a baby reptile or bird comes out.

internal organs (in-TUR-nuhl OR-guhns): Body parts, such as the heart and lungs, that are inside the body.

predators (PRED-uh-turs): Animals that live by hunting other animals for food.

Index

bones 21, 22
cold blooded 4, 6
eggs 16, 19
skin 11, 12
tail(s) 15

Websites to Visit

http://a-z-animals.com/animals/iguana
http://animals.sandiegozoo.org/animals/iguana
www.ducksters.com/animals/green_iguana.php

About the Author

Darla Duhaime is fascinated by all the cool things animals and people can do. When she's not writing books for kids, she enjoys eating strange foods, daydreaming, and cloud-watching. She likes to stay active and is known for keeping things interesting at family gatherings.

Meet The Author!
www.meetREMauthors.com

© 2017 Rourke Educational Media

All rights reserved. No part of this book may be reproduced or utilized in any form or by any means, electronic or mechanical including photocopying, recording, or by any information storage and retrieval system without permission in writing from the publisher.

www.rourkeeducationalmedia.com

PHOTO CREDITS: Cover © Gaschwald-Shutterstock; title page © Hanoi Photography; page 5 © JonGorr; page 7 © Flavio Vallenari; page 8 © somplyzel; page 10 © 101cats; page 13 © PeterVrabel; page 14 © Bariscan Celik; page 17 © bluedog studio; page 18 © piccaya; page 20 © Kharkovalex; page 22 © JBryson

Edited by: Keli Sipperley
Cover design by: Nicola Stratford - www.nicolastratford.com
Interior design by: Jen Thomas

Library of Congress PCN Data

Iguanas/ Darla Duhaime
(Reptiles)
ISBN (hard cover)(alk. paper) 978-1-68342-158-0
ISBN (soft cover) 978-1-68342-200-6
ISBN (e-Book) 978-1-68342-228-0
Library of Congress Control Number: 2016956515

Printed in the United States of America, North Mankato, Minnesota

Also Available as:
ROURKE'S
e-Books